Children's books. Poems.
ISBN: 979-1-7777665-0-4
Published by Douglas Cochran

Dedication

To Rory and Audrey, may you grow up loving nature and the wonders that it holds.

Thanks to Lizzy Cochran for editing.

Graphic design by Sherry Matthews

A howling owl can be quite fowl
But mostly they're majestic.

In graceful flight, daytime or night
More daring than domestic

Bobby **B**ear has no real cares
At least his cares are sparing
He lumbers round, makes growling sounds
His way of bearly sharing

Chipmunk likes to check you out
He's a checking chipmunk chum
But soon he's back to storing nuts
To munch when winter comes

Red-eye Duck has all the luck
He's handsome and delightful
He poses while you snap his pic
Looking quite insightful

An **E**agle is a fearsome bird
Two are twice as awesome
They poise for their chance to strike
One drab day in the autumn

Fox is so furry, funny and fast
Whenever he races, he never comes last
But when he rests he rests with the best
For the test of the rest is to never be stressed

Grizzly Gus makes no fuss
When he washes in the water
He likes to get his fur all clean
Cause that is what he'd druther

Harry Hawk, sees a whole lot
As he studies his surroundings
Like where's a lair where he can snare
A meal of little groundlings

Itsy bitsy humming bird
Takes a little break
To rest her tiny beating heart
Before it starts to ache

There's a Jay in my way
Perhaps I should be movin'
She may just land onto my hand
If that is what she's choosin'

Kings of birds gaze undisturbed
Spying from their perches
They hope to see a meal revealed
And triumph from their searches

Once there was a Ladybug
More bug than she was lady
She ate her weight in tender leaves
And tended to her babies

This Macaque is a monkey
Who hangs out in Japan
He fills his cheeks up with treats
And chews them when he can

Now they're nestled nicely
This family cuddles tight
A cozy time for snoozing
In daytime or at night

Spot these Otters on the land
They neither run nor hurry
They're safe at sea where they'll be
If ever they must scurry

Piggy Porker pokes the earth
Pursuing Piggy's passion
Perhaps he'll prod a truffle out
In perfect piggy fashion

Three quick Quackers walking in a row
Said the first quick quacker, *where shall we go?*
The second quick quacker said, *how would I know?*
I'm just a happy quacker going with the flow.

Rachael Rabbit's a creature of habit
Refined and oh so gentle
She delights to chew on grassy dew
For reasons sentimental

Shirley seal's delightfully real,
She brims with curiosity
Up! she pops from the sea
With no hint of animosity

Murtle Turtle isn't purple
She blends into the sea
She cruises down below the waves
Then surfaces to breathe

Look at Us, we make no fuss
So different but complimental
One rides behind, and doesn't mind
If there's a toot, quite accidental

Very wise, with piercing eyes
Baby monkey munches
As he does please, he chews on leaves
For breakfast or for brunches

Woodpecker, Woodpecker
Whack away on wood
Why would you want to?
Just 'cause you could

Xtraordinary point of view
So very calm and caring
There's more horse than this, of course
In her majestic bearing

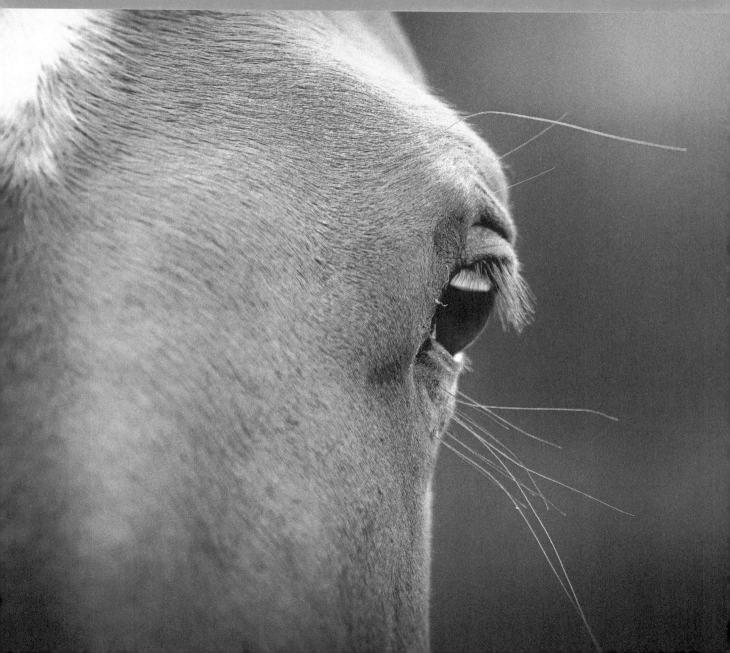

Yelling like a Mongoose
Is frightening as can be
I would cuddle up to him
If he'd stop scaring me

Zoos are full of animals
Many more live in the wild
Sometimes while you're watching them
They watch you, quite beguiled

About the Author

Douglas Cochran is a semi-retired lawyer and adjudicator living in Vancouver, B.C. He conceived of this book for his two grandchildren, Rory and Audrey. Douglas is new to writing childrens' books, with one other title, The Hyrax in the Mogogos available directly through dclaw1@telus.net or Amazon books. More information about Douglas' writing and art can be found at www.dougsneon.ca.

Photography

Nik Cochran is a software developer with a passion for wildlife photography, living in Vancouver, Canada. You can find more of his photography at his website niks.blog or on Instagram @nikcochran.

Author's note: Please forgive me for taking poetic liberties in the naming of animals and with my relaxed approach to grammatical convention. It's all in good fun.